Written by Tim Kennington
Illustrated by Josy Bloggs
Edited by Emma Taylor
Designed by Jake Da'Costa
Cover design by John Bigwood

BRILLIANT
BODIES
INSIDE AND OUT

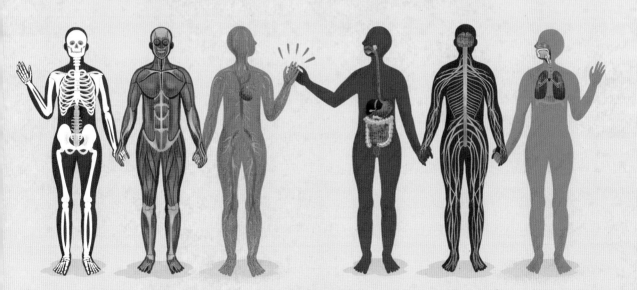

BUSTER BOOKS

First published in Great Britain in 2024 by Buster Books, an imprint of
Michael O'Mara Books Limited, 9 Lion Yard, Tremadoc Road, London SW4 7NQ

W www.mombooks.com/buster   f Buster Books   🐦 @BusterBooks   📷 @buster_books

ISBN: 978-1-78055-889-9

1 3 5 7 9 10 8 6 4 2

This book was printed in February 2024 by Leo Paper Products Ltd,
Heshan Astros Printing Limited, Xuantan Temple Industrial Zone,
Gulao Town, Heshan City, Guangdong Province, China.

BRILLIANT
BODIES
INSIDE AND OUT

CONTENTS

INTRODUCTION

Bodies are amazing things – from the human body to fascinating animal bodies, this book will reveal their secrets, inside and out.

Discover more about your awesome body parts, from the hair on your head to the nails on your toes. Find out surprising facts about animal bodies, such as the super sight of a bald eagle and the incredible strength of a dung beetle. All of the creatures inside this book will blow your mind.

People have been studying bodies for thousands of years and scientists are still making loads of new discoveries about them. So it's time to meet some brilliant bodies!

If you come across any words you don't know, don't worry. Check out the Glossary on page 92, where some of the harder words are explained.

Any time you see this icon, it means there's something for you to try yourself at home.

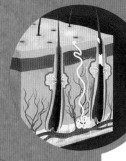

1

BODY BASICS

Your brilliant body is what allows you to do every single thing that you do, every day. From remembering what you learnt at school and eating a tasty meal to watching your favourite TV show and dancing along to a song – it's responsible for everything.

Your body is made up of thousands of different parts that all work together. These parts can be put into groups called 'systems'. There are six main systems you'll be introduced to, but before you start exploring each of them, here are some body basics you should know. This chapter is all about the differences between human bodies and how they're made, from the different layers of your skin to how you move your muscles.

THE BODY'S SYSTEMS
WORKING TOGETHER

The groups of organs and tissues that work together inside your body are called 'systems'. Here are the six main systems and what they do.

SKELETAL

Your bones, ligaments and cartilage help to shape and support your body.

See pages 50–57.

MUSCULAR

Your muscles and tendons help you to move your body.

See pages 22–23.

CIRCULATORY

Your heart and blood vessels keep your blood flowing around your body.

See pages 64–69.

INCREDIBLE SYSTEMS

Your body could not survive without all of these systems.
They rely on each other to function and are constantly
passing instructions to one another.

Think of your body like a computer, running lots of different
programs all at once to keep it working at its best.

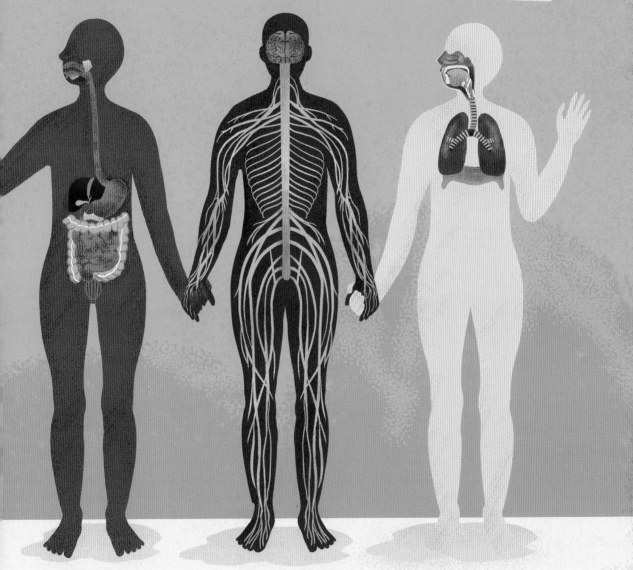

DIGESTIVE

Your mouth and guts
help you to eat and
digest your food.

See pages 70–81.

NERVOUS

Your brain, spinal cord and
nerves send information
to the different parts
of your body.

See pages 40–49.

RESPIRATORY

Your airways and
lungs help you
to breathe.

See pages 60–63.

DIFFERENT BODIES
GENITALIA, HORMONES AND GENDER

Human bodies are mostly the same from person to person. The differences between them are only small, such as eye and skin colour, allergies and illnesses, and varying abilities. The main difference between bodies is whether they have male or female genitalia.

GENITALIA

Genitalia is the group of body parts that are used to create new life.

Male genitalia, such as the testicles, need to be kept cool, so are on the outside of the body. Female genitalia, such as the ovaries, require warmth and so are deep inside the body. These different temperatures keep them working properly.

The diagrams below show the male and female parts.

HORMONES

Hormones are chemicals that bodies make in order to do certain things.

Testosterone is the main sex hormone in male bodies, which is responsible for puberty and helping to make sperm.

The main sex hormones in female bodies are oestrogen and progesterone, which are responsible for puberty, menstruation and pregnancy.

GENDER

When you're born, you're given a gender: male or female. This is determined by whether you have male or female genitalia.

Not everyone feels their gender is the same as the one they're given at birth. Some people feel female with a male body, some people feel male with a female body, and some people don't feel male or female at all.

All bodies are different, and the one you're born with is only a small part of the amazing things that make you who you are.

FEMALE GENITALIA

1. OVARIES
Organs that store and release eggs. They also produce oestrogen and progesterone.

2. FALLOPIAN TUBES
Tubes that connect the ovaries to the uterus. They're also where eggs are fertilized.

3. UTERUS
Where fertilized eggs grow.

4. CERVIX
The opening of the uterus.

5. VAGINA
A passageway that connects the uterus with the outside of the body.

MALE GENITALIA

1. TESTICLES
Skin-covered balls that hang beneath the penis. They produce testosterone and make sperm.

2. PENIS
A spongy piece of tissue that sticks out from between the legs. It carries sperm out of the body.

3. URETHRA
A long tube that carries urine (wee) through the penis and out of the body.

WHERE DO BODIES COME FROM?

HOW LIFE BEGINS

Did you know that your body began as a single cell? Discover how it grew and developed in the 40 weeks before you were born.

1. FERTILIZATION

Once a month, an egg is released from one of the two ovaries. During sexual intercourse, a penis releases sperm into the vagina. Only a few sperm make it to the fallopian tubes and, usually, just one fertilizes an egg.

When the sperm reaches the egg, it releases chemicals from its head that help it to break through the egg's surface. Once inside, it loses its tail and joins together with the egg's nucleus (centre).

EGG

NUCLEUS

SPERM

SPERM

HEAD
Contains chromosomes.
See pages 18–19.

TAIL
Pushes the sperm towards the egg.

MIDDLE
Gives the sperm energy to move.

2. CELL DIVISION

Almost a day and a half after fertilization, the egg divides into two joined cells.

After three days, as the egg travels along one of the fallopian tubes towards the uterus, it splits again, eight times, into 16 cells.

The egg continues to split and develops into a cluster of lots of cells, called a blastocyst.

3. IMPLANTATION

The blastocyst attaches itself to the lining of the uterus, where it grows into an embryo.

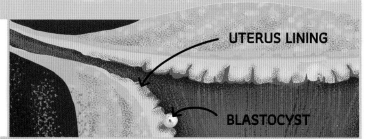

UTERUS LINING

BLASTOCYST

4. GROWING A FOETUS

Around eight weeks after fertilization, the growing baby is now called a foetus. It has a large head with a developing brain, as well as fingers and toes. It grows stronger and becomes more active.

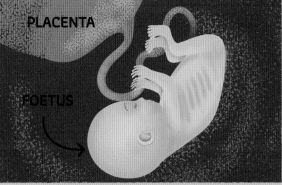

PLACENTA

FOETUS

5. BIRTH

After about nine months of growing inside the uterus, the baby is ready to be born.

PLACENTA
Links the mother's blood supply to the baby.

UTERUS WALL
Protects the baby during pregnancy.

UMBILICAL CORD
Connects the baby to the placenta and delivers nutrients from the mother.

BIRTH CANAL
Widens to allow the baby to be pushed through the vagina. Sometimes, this is not possible and an operation is needed to remove the baby. This is called a Caesarean section.

DID YOU KNOW?

If there is no fertilized egg, the lining of the uterus breaks down and exits the body as blood. This is called a period or menstruation.

GROWING BODIES

HOW YOUR BODY GROWS AND SHRINKS

Human bodies experience lots of changes as they grow. Here's a look at some of the ways they develop throughout a lifetime.

BABIES

After babies are born, they continue to grow about 2 centimetres (0.79 inches) a month. They change on the inside, too, as some of their bones fuse (join) together and form their full skeleton.

CHILDREN

Children aged between six and 12 grow at a fairly constant speed, which is about 6–7 cm (2.5 in) a year. So your body is 6 cm taller than it was last year and 6 cm shorter than it will be next year.

TEENAGERS

During the change from childhood to adulthood, teenagers go through 'puberty'. This is when their reproductive systems start to develop, preparing to make babies. Teenagers' bodies become hairier and sweatier, too.

DIVIDING CELLS

When you're a baby, your cells divide and multiply at a fast rate so that your body can develop. However, when you reach adulthood, your cells stop dividing for growth and instead divide to replace old or damaged cells, and at a slower rate.

GROWN-UPS

After puberty, people's bodies stop growing and this is the tallest they'll ever be. However, their brain will keep developing until they're around 25 years old. Around the age of 30, their muscles will gradually start to weaken and fertility (the ability to have babies) also starts to decline.

OLDER PEOPLE

After the age of 40, the body slowly starts getting smaller. At 70, this process speeds up. This is to do with the spine, which is made up of lots of little bones called vertebrae. Between these bones are discs made of soft tissue, which is mostly water. As people get older, the discs lose water, which makes them thinner. All of these discs add up to make a quarter of the height of the spine so it's noticeable when each of them shrinks, even just a little bit.

DNA AND CHROMOSOMES

WHY DO YOU LOOK THE WAY YOU LOOK?

All of the information about how your body looks and works is carried
in a chemical substance called deoxyribonucleic acid (DNA).
This is found inside the nucleus of every cell in your body.

DNA

DNA contains all of the information about how your
body should look and work. This ranges from your hair
colour to what your earlobes look like, and even if you
can naturally roll your tongue. Each bit of information is
carried by different sections of the DNA, called genes.
Other than identical twins, no two people in the
world have exactly the same DNA and genes.

CHROMOSOMES

Your DNA and genes are stored in tiny structures called chromosomes, which come in pairs. There are 46 chromosomes inside the nucleus of each cell: 23 come from your mother and 23 from your father.

Usually, the pairs look the same, but there is one pair that appears different for bodies that have either male or female genitalia. Female bodies have two of the same type of chromosome (XX) and male bodies have two different types of chromosome (XY).

DOUBLE HELIX
The spiral structure of DNA. It is made up of chemical substances that link together like a chain.

DID YOU KNOW?

One of the strangest genes is called OR6A2. It controls part of your senses that can detect chemicals found in soap and herbs, such as coriander. But OR6A2 doesn't appear in everybody's DNA. If you have it, you probably don't like coriander because this gene makes it smell funny and taste like soap!

ANIMAL DNA

Every living organism on the planet has DNA and you share a large part of your DNA with lots of other animals.

Your DNA is ...

• 98.8% the same as a chimpanzee
• 98% the same as a pig
• 80% the same as a cow
• 70% the same as a slug

NAILS AND HAIR

THE BODY'S PROTECTION

It might seem odd to put nails and hair together as they don't look anything alike. However, they're actually quite similar and are made of the same material — a protein called keratin.

NAILS

The ends of your fingers and toes are very sensitive, so your nails act like shields and protect them. Fingernails also help you to grip and pick up small objects.

Your nails start growing from the root, under the surface of your skin. New cells push out old cells, which harden and die. The newly formed nails slide out through the cuticles and form the nail plate. Your nails grow at around 3.5 millimetres (0.14 in) a month.

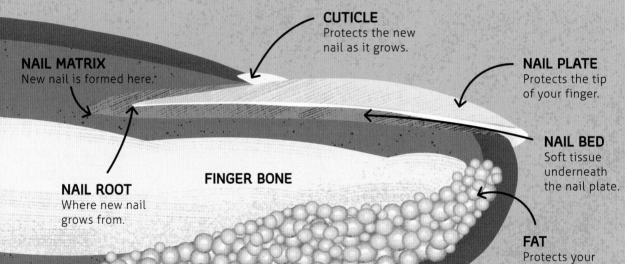

CUTICLE
Protects the new nail as it grows.

NAIL MATRIX
New nail is formed here.

NAIL PLATE
Protects the tip of your finger.

NAIL BED
Soft tissue underneath the nail plate.

FINGER BONE

NAIL ROOT
Where new nail grows from.

FAT
Protects your finger bone.

DEAD OR ALIVE?

Nails and hair are actually dead cells. Don't worry – they're not zombies! They've just been pushed out by the living roots underneath your skin.

It's just as well your visible nails and hair are dead, otherwise it would really hurt whenever you cut them!

HAIR

Your hair grows from tiny holes under the skin called follicles. Blood vessels at the base of these follicles feed the hair roots nutrients to keep them growing. As your hairs travel through the skin, they get coated in oils which make them shiny.

Your body is covered in about 5 million hair follicles. There are approximately 100,000 hair follicles on your scalp, which grow around 12.7 mm (0.5 in) a month.

GETTING OLDER

Not all of your follicles are growing hair all of the time. Some of them take breaks, which can last several months, and then the hair falls out. You lose about 50 to 100 hairs every day.

As you get older, these breaks become longer. For some people, the follicles stop making hairs altogether and they start to go bald.

Hairs also lose their colour as people age. The amount of pigment in the hair follicles reduces and the hairs go grey or white.

DID YOU KNOW?

The world record for the longest fingernails on a single hand belongs to Shridhar Chillal, who grew his for 66 years. If you put all of the nails on his left hand together and measured them, they'd be over 9 metres (29.5 feet) long.

SKELETAL MUSCLES

HOW YOUR BONES AND SKELETAL MUSCLES WORK TOGETHER

Your body is covered in skeletal muscles, which pull on your bones to move your skeleton. Here's how these muscles work.

OPPOSITE PAIRS

Your skeletal muscles work in opposite pairs. When you bend your arm, your tricep stretches out and relaxes while your bicep squeezes in and contracts. The bulge that appears towards the top of your arm is the squashed muscle of your bicep. When you straighten your arm, your muscles do the opposite, so your tricep squeezes in and contracts while your bicep relaxes.

TENDONS

Tendons are flexible cords that connect your muscles to the bones they pull and can be found all over your body. For example, when you squeeze your arm muscles, the tendon pulls on the bone of your arm, causing it to move.

OTHER TYPES

Your other muscles include smooth muscle, such as that inside your stomach and intestines, which pushes food through your body. You also have cardiac (heart) muscle, which keeps your heart beating.

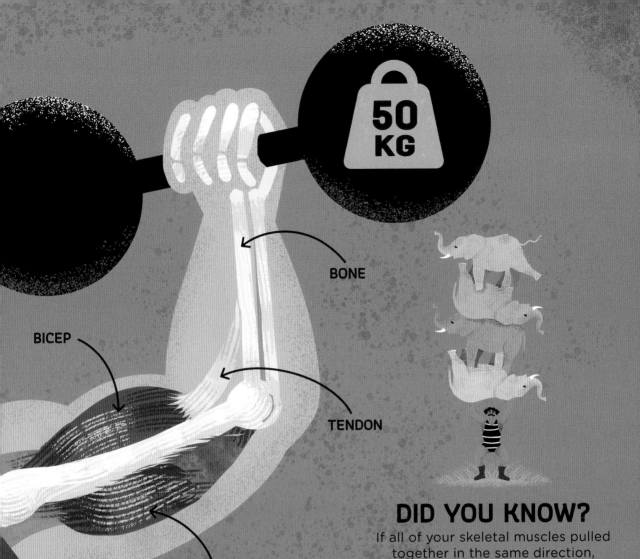

BONE

BICEP

TENDON

TRICEP

DID YOU KNOW?

If all of your skeletal muscles pulled together in the same direction, you'd be able to lift 25 tonnes (27.6 tons). That's the same weight as four African elephants!

WIGGLE, WIGGLE

All of your skeletal muscles are connected to bone at both ends, except for one – your tongue! This is known as a muscular hydrostat, which means it can wiggle around in lots of impressive ways. Another example of a muscular hydrostat is an octopus's arm, which moves in exactly the same way as your tongue.

SKIN DEEP
THE BODY'S OUTER BARRIER

Your skin is the largest organ in your body. It's made up of millions of tiny cells, which cover and help to protect everything inside it.

INSIDE YOUR SKIN

Your skin consists of three layers, which all do different jobs:

1. EPIDERMIS

Your skin cells are continuously making new cells. This process starts at the base of your outer layer of skin. The cells then travel up to the surface, which can take about a month. While they're travelling, old cells fall off. Every year, you can lose an average of 525 grams (1.2 pounds) of skin – that's almost the same weight as three hamsters.

2. DERMIS

This layer is packed with nerves, the endings of which sense pain, pressure and temperature. These nerves send information about what you can feel to your brain. The dermis also contains sweat glands, which release moisture through your pores on to the surface of your skin to help keep you cool.

3. HYPODERMIS

This stores energy and keeps body heat in. It also protects your organs, muscles and bones.

SEBACEOUS GLAND
Creates and releases sebum.

SWEAT PORE
Releases sweat.

SEBUM
Skin's natural oil.

NERVE
Carries signals from touch sensors to the brain.

BLOOD VESSELS
Supply oxygen and nutrients to the skin.

SWEAT GLAND
Releases moisture on to the skin's surface.

HAIR FOLLICLE
Hairs grow out of pocket called follicle

MELANIN

While most of your skin is busy producing new cells, a small part of it is also making a substance called melanin. This helps to protect your body from the ultraviolet rays in sunlight, which can cause damage to the skin. Melanin creates different skin colours, and the more melanin you have the darker your skin is and the more protected you are from the Sun.

Most people's skin darkens when exposed to ultraviolet rays. However, no amount of melanin can fully protect you from the Sun's rays.

STAY SAFE IN THE SUN

- Cover as much of your skin as possible. A T-shirt and hat are essential.

- Put on sun cream with at least SPF 30 and reapply every two hours.

- Keep cool in the shade during the hottest parts of the day: between 11 am and 3 pm.

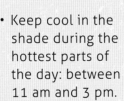

DID YOU KNOW?

Shark skin may look smooth, but it's covered in tiny V-shaped scales called dermal denticles, which look like teeth when viewed under a microscope. These scales help sharks to swim quickly through the water by reducing friction.

OPEN WIDE
THE DIFFERENT TYPES OF TEETH

Your teeth are an important part of both your skeletal system and your digestive system. They help to break down your food into manageable pieces that you can swallow and then digest.

INSIDE A TOOTH

The part of your tooth that you can see is called the crown, which is coated in a substance called enamel. Beneath this is 'dentine', which is harder than bone and forms the main part of your tooth. The diagram below shows the different types of teeth inside an adult's mouth and what they do.

CROWN — ← ENAMEL
← DENTINE
ROOT —

INCISORS
Chop and cut your food into small pieces.

CANINES
Pierce and tear your food, as they often have a sharp, pointed edge.

MOLARS
Grind and mash your food.

PREMOLARS
Crush and grind your food.

WISDOM TEETH
These teeth are molars, which grind up food. They're the last to grow and don't usually appear until you're around 17–21 years old, although some people never develop them. Most adults have between 28 and 32 teeth.

● Incisor
● Canine
● Premolar
● Molar

MILK TEETH

You are born with all of your teeth already inside your skull, hidden inside your gums. Your first set of teeth are called your preliminary or milk teeth. When you're around five or six years old, adult teeth start to push up out of your jawbone and wear away the root of your milk teeth. This process makes them wobbly and fall out, giving your adult ones room to grow.

DID YOU KNOW?

The animal with the most teeth isn't a shark, lion or piranha, but a snail! Its radula (tongue) has up to 12,000 teeth which work like a cheese-grater, scraping off little bits of leaf as its body moves over them.

GAP TEETH

If you have a gap between your teeth, then you have what's called a diastema. It's most noticeable between your incisors.

Herbivores (plant-eating animals) often have them, too, between their front and back teeth to help move food inside their cheeks. This means they can continue feeding without taking lots of breaks.

YOUR SENSES

Your body is covered in sensors that detect the world around you.

You have five main sense organs, which include your eyes, ears, nose, tongue and skin. These organs collect information, and sensory cells – or receptors – pass it to your brain through the nerves in your body. Your brain processes the information and then tells the body how to react to it.

Your senses can help you to spot danger, so they're very important for keeping you safe. In this chapter, you'll discover the different parts of each sense organ and how they work.

HOW YOU SEE
THE SCIENCE OF SIGHT

You use your eyes and your brain to see. Your eyes detect light that is reflected off the objects around you. Signals are then sent to your brain, which helps you to understand what this light means, creating a 3D colour image of what's in front of you.

IRIS
The coloured part of your eye, which controls how much light enters the pupil.

PUPIL
The opening of the iris, which lets light inside. When there's lots of light, your pupil gets smaller to stop too much light entering and damaging your eye. When there's not enough light, it gets larger to let more light inside.

RETINA
A layer at the back of your eye that receives images and sends them to the brain as electrical signals. It's covered in light-detecting cells called rods and cones. Rods help you to see the shape of objects when it's dark, and cones help you to see colour and detail.

CORNEA
A clear layer of tissue that covers your eye. It lets light in and helps to focus it.

LENS
The lens focuses light to make sure it hits your retina at the back of your eye.

VITREOUS HUMOR
A clear, gel-like substance that helps to maintain the round shape of your eye.

BLOOD VESSELS
These carry oxygen and nutrients to the eye.

OPTIC NERVE
Nerve fibres that carry electrical signals from the retina to the brain to be processed.

GLASSES

For some people, the light coming into the eye doesn't hit the retina in the right place, so this makes things hard to see. A pair of glasses acts like another lens and works with your eyes to help bend the light so that it hits the right spot.

Short-sighted people struggle to focus on things in the distance as they appear blurry. Long-sighted people find it difficult to focus on things close up, which means activities such as reading can be hard to do without glasses.

TRY IT AT HOME: BLIND SPOT TEST

Everyone has a blind spot in each eye. This is a small area at the back of your eye where there are no light-detecting cells so your retina can't see. To test your blind spot, hold the book at arm's length, cover your left eye and stare at the cross. Slowly move the book towards you and the black star on the right will disappear for a second. This is caused by the light from it falling on your blind spot.

$$ + \qquad\qquad ★ $$

NIGHT VISION

Some animals can see in the dark because they have more rods in their retinas than humans. Behind their retinas, they also have another layer called a 'tapetum lucidum', which reflects light back, giving the rods a second chance to sense light. This is why their eyes appear to shine or glow in the dark.

Most animals that have this extra layer are mammals, such as cats. It's especially useful to nocturnal animals that hunt at night.

HOW YOU HEAR
SOUND'S INCREDIBLE JOURNEY

Sounds are vibrations that travel through the air as waves. These waves are collected by your ear and transformed into electrical signals that are sent along nerves to your brain, which interprets them as sounds. The diagram below shows the different parts of your ear and how vibrations travel through it.

OUTER EAR
This acts like a funnel, channelling vibrations in the air inside your ear.

EAR CANAL
About the width of a pencil, the ear canal carries sound waves towards the eardrum.

EARDRUM
A small, thin layer of skin that stretches across the ear canal. It acts like a drum, vibrating when hit by sound waves.

EAR BONES
The smallest bones inside your body, which are named after their shapes: the hammer, anvil and stirrup. When the eardrum vibrates, it causes these three bones to move, transmitting the vibration further inside the ear.

COCHLEA
This is filled with tiny hair cells that detect incoming vibrations, and fluid, which moves in response to the vibrations. As the fluid moves, nerve endings transform the vibrations into electrical impulses that travel along the cochlear nerve to the brain.

OVAL WINDOW
A thin skin-like membrane, which is the entrance to the inner ear, known as the cochlea.

EUSTACHIAN TUBE
This drains fluid from the ear into the throat.

We measure the loudness of sounds in decibels (dB). Your normal talking voice is around 60 dB, but a sperm whale is capable of producing clicking sounds of up to 233 dB. This makes it the loudest animal on the planet.

TRY IT AT HOME: MAKE A STRING PHONE

Sound vibrations travel better through solid objects than they do through air. This is because the particles of a solid object are packed together more tightly than the particles in the air and so can transmit the vibrations faster. To test this, try the activity below:

1. Using a sharp pencil, make a hole in the bottom of two paper cups.

2. Thread a long piece of string through the holes in each cup. Then, secure the string inside each cup with a knot.

3. Give one cup to a friend and walk away from one another until the string is pulled tight.

4. Put your cup over your ear while your friend talks into the other cup. You should be able to hear them. Pretty cool, right?

HOW YOU SMELL

GET A WHIFF OF THIS ...

Your nose is a passageway for air to get into your lungs, but it's also how you smell. Smell receptors inside your nose detect odours in the air. Nerves then carry signals from these smell receptors to your brain to be processed. The diagram below shows the main parts of the nose and what they do.

OLFACTORY NERVES
These carry signals from smell receptors to the olfactory bulb.

OLFACTORY BULB
Messages from the olfactory nerves are sent from the olfactory bulb to the brain for processing.

OLFACTORY EPITHELIUM
At the top of the nasal cavity there are millions of smell receptor cells that can detect more than 1 trillion different smells.

NASAL CAVITY
Inside the nasal cavity, the air is filtered, warmed and moistened before entering the lungs.

MUCOUS MEMBRANE
This produces a slimy substance called mucus, which catches dust and other small particles that can irritate your lungs. Tiny hairs called cilia help to push the mucus towards the nose or throat so that it drains out.

NOSTRILS
The two openings of the nose.

CAN'T SMELL?

Just like some people can't see or hear, there are those who can't smell. This is a condition called anosmia, which can occur when the mucous membrane is irritated or blocked. This can be temporary, such as when you have a really bad cold or hay fever, or it can be permanent.

BLOODHOUNDS

Bloodhounds have an incredible sense of smell. Inside their nose, they have around 300 million smell receptors. They can follow a scent trail for more than 209 kilometres (130 miles) and track a scent that's more than 12 days old! Their sense of smell is so reliable that their findings can be used in some US law courts.

ACHOO!

DID YOU KNOW?

Sneezes can travel up to 160 km (100 mi) per hour. That's 40 km (25 mi) an hour faster than the top speed of a cheetah!

HUW YOU TASTE

TAKE A TOUR OF YOUR TONGUE

Your tongue is a muscle packed with thousands of taste buds that can recognize different tastes. Here are the main parts of the tongue and what they do.

PAPILLAE
Your tongue is covered in tiny bumps called papillae. Pointy ones help the tongue to grip food while you're chewing and round ones contain taste buds.

TASTE BUDS
Saliva dissolves the particles of the food you eat, which then enter the taste buds.

TASTE HAIRS
These taste the food.

TASTE RECEPTOR CELLS
These detect the flavour of food, such as if it's sweet, salty or sour.

NERVE FIBRES
These carry information from receptor cells in the taste buds to the brain.

SLURRP!

TYPES OF TASTE

You're born with thousands of taste buds. As you age, you can lose over half of them. This change can explain why some foods, in particular bitter-tasting foods, might taste stronger to you than to an adult. With fewer taste buds, flavours can taste weaker.

Your taste buds are able to pick up five main types of taste:
SWEET = fruits and sweets
SOUR = vinegar and lemons
SALTY = crisps and bacon
BITTER = broccoli and sesame seeds
UMAMI (SAVOURY) = mushrooms and aged cheese, such as parmesan.

WHAT'S YOUR FLAVOUR?

The overall flavour of a food comes from a combination of its taste, smell, texture and temperature, so how you experience taste is affected by your other senses, too. For example, some people think that crisps with a louder crunch taste better than those without and that brightly coloured drinks taste nicer.

TRY IT AT HOME: TASTE TEST

Your sense of smell is 10,000 times more sensitive than your sense of taste. To put this to the test, follow the instructions below:

1. Blindfold a friend and ask them to pinch their nose closed.

2. Feed them some different-tasting foods, such as cheese, fruit and chocolate, and see if they can guess what they are.

3. Now try it again with their nose unpinched. It should be a lot easier!

DID YOU KNOW?

Catfish have the strongest sense of taste in the animal kingdom. Their entire bodies are covered in thousands of taste receptor cells so that they can detect when a tasty meal is nearby. This sense is essential for their survival in the murky rivers where they hunt.

HOW YOU FEEL

TOUCH SENSORS

Your skin is packed with millions of touch sensors that detect different sensations and help you to feel the things around you. Sensory nerves inside the skin carry signals from these touch sensors to the brain to be processed.

TYPES OF TOUCH

Different touch sensors respond to different sensations. The diagram below shows where these touch sensors are located in your skin.

MERKEL'S DISCS
Detect levels of light and medium pressure, such as someone tapping you on the arm or back.

RUFFINI ENDINGS
Sense your skin being squeezed or stretched.

MEISSENER'S CORPUSCLES
Detect very light touch, such as being tickled by a feather.

FREE NERVE ENDINGS
Respond to pain, light touch and feeling hot or cold.

PACINIAN CORPUSCLES
Respond to deep pressure, such as a big, warm hug and vibrations.

OUCH!

It's important that you're able to feel pain as it can act as a warning when you're in danger. For example, the sensation of burning your tongue on a hot slice of pizza stops you from eating it before you cause yourself more harm, even if it's really tasty ...

SQUASHED NERVES

Sensory nerves send information to your brain using tiny electrical signals. If a nerve gets squashed by pressure, it can be hard for these electrical signals to get through. After a while, the electrical charge builds up and you might feel a strange, numbing sensation – scientists call this paresthesia.

The feeling of pins and needles is a sign of your nerves waking up and suddenly sending and receiving lots of signals. This is why it feels so uncomfortable – it's a sensory overload!

TRY IT AT HOME: THE PAPER-CLIP TEST

Different parts of your body have different amounts of sensory nerves. Your fingertips have a lot more than your elbow, which is why they're able to notice gentler touches. To put this to the test, follow the steps below:

1. Unbend a paper clip and rebend it into a U-shape.

2. Ask a friend to close their eyes and touch their palm with the two points of the paper clip. They should be able to feel both points.

3. Next, try testing a part of the body that's less sensitive, such as their back. It should be harder for them to feel both points of the clip and they may only feel one.

4. If they can still feel both, pinch the points closer together so that the gap is smaller, and then try again. What can they feel?

DID YOU KNOW?

Seals have incredibly sensitive whiskers that can detect underwater vibrations from other animals. Experiments have shown that their whiskers are capable of sensing fish from 100 m (328 ft) away.

3

THE NERVOUS SYSTEM

Your nervous system controls everything you do, from breathing and walking to thinking and feeling. It's made up of your brain, spinal cord and a network of nerves that branch out to every part of your body. Via the spinal cord, these nerves send messages between your body and brain as tiny pulses of electricity.

Your brain is the nervous system's control centre. On receiving messages from other parts of your body, it tells them what to do.

Turn the page to explore the different parts of your nervous system and find out what they do.

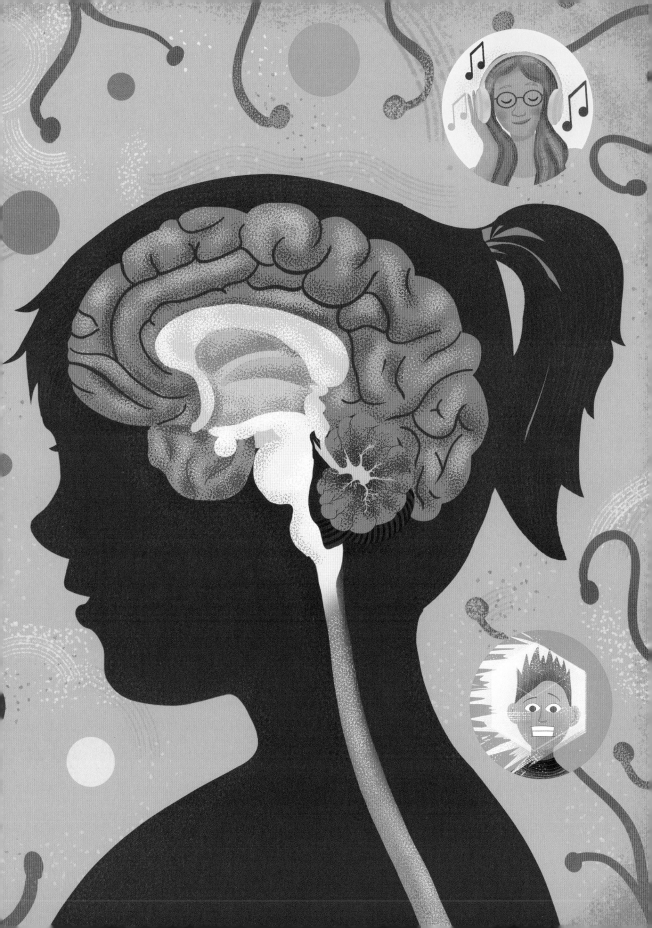

BRAIN BASICS

AN INTRODUCTION TO YOUR BRAIN

Your brain is your most complicated organ and the control centre of your entire body. This diagram shows its main parts and what they do.

CEREBRUM
The largest and most powerful part of your brain, which is responsible for all of your thoughts, memories and emotions. It also helps you to communicate and solve problems.

It has grooves and folds called gyri, which increase the surface area, allowing more brain cells to be stored. *See pages 44–45.*

BRAINSTEM
This connects your brain to your spinal cord. It controls basic functions that you probably don't even notice happening, such as breathing and swallowing food.

CEREBELLUM
This controls some of your body's movement and ability to balance. It's particularly helpful with movements that need practice, such as riding a bicycle or playing a musical instrument. Through repeated actions, your cerebellum gets used to the motions and so they become smoother and more effortless.

SPINAL CORD
This carries information between your brain and your body. *See pages 46–47.*

HOW BIG IS YOUR BRAIN?

To find out how big your brain is, make fists with both your hands and hold them together. Your two fists are around the same size and shape as your brain.

A fully grown brain weighs around 1.3 kg (2.9 lb). That's roughly the same weight as two basketballs or 62 mice.

ROARR!

UNBELIEVABLE BRAINS

The biggest brain in the animal kingdom weighs around 8 kg (17.6 lb) and belongs to the sperm whale. On the other hand, experts estimate that a T. rex, which had a skull over 1.5 m (4.9 ft) long, had a brain around a third the size of an adult human's. It's believed it could have weighed between 350 g (0.8 lb) and 1 kg (2.2 lb).

BRAIN FREEZE

Have you ever eaten something cold too quickly and felt like your brain is freezing over? Scientists think that this aching sensation is caused by your blood vessels suddenly changing size. Blood vessels in your mouth expand to push blood to the cold area to heat it up. The rapid expansion of your blood vessels and the increased blood flow is what causes this little pain sensation.

A LOOK AT YOUR LOBES

INSIDE YOUR CEREBRUM

Your cerebrum is made up of lots of areas called lobes, which are constantly passing information to one another. This collection of lobes is also known as the cerebral cortex. Here's a closer look at the four main lobes.

FRONTAL LOBE
Controls the movements your body makes, such as running and jumping. It's also responsible for your ability to concentrate, your long-term memories and your speech.

TEMPORAL LOBE
This is responsible for helping you to understand what you read and hear, including making sense of written and spoken language. It also contains the 'hippocampus', which helps you to learn and remember facts.

MEMORY

BODY TEMPERATURE

TOUCH

TASTE

JUMPING

TALKING

MUSIC

CONVERSATION

READING

RIGHT OR LEFT?

Your cerebrum is divided into two halves called hemispheres. The right hemisphere controls the left side of the body and is responsible for creative and emotional impulses. The left hemisphere controls the right side of the body and is in charge of verbal and written skills, as well as dealing with numbers and problem-solving.

PARIETAL LOBE

Helps you to understand all of the information you get from your nerves. It processes sensory information to do with touch, taste and temperature.

OCCIPITAL LOBE

This is in charge of processing what your eyes see. It helps you to understand different shapes, distances and colours.

DISTANCE

COLOUR

CLARK'S NUTCRACKER

DID YOU KNOW?

The Clark's nutcracker is a type of crow with an incredible memory. It buries at least 30,000 nuts and seeds in thousands of locations and is able to find them up to nine months after storing them. This is thanks to its hippocampus, which is larger than those of other nutcracker birds.

YOUR SPINAL CORD

BRAIN'S BEST FRIEND

Your spinal cord carries information between your brain and your body. It's made up of nerve tissues containing millions of nerve cells called neurons, which transport electrical signals. The diagram below shows the main parts of the spinal cord and what they do.

WHAT'S THE MATTER?

This diagram shows what the inside of the spinal cord would look like if it were cut in half.

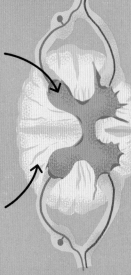

WHITE MATTER

GREY MATTER

In the centre, there is a section called grey matter, which is in the shape of a butterfly. The top of each 'wing' processes sensory information from the body and the bottom of each 'wing' sends out signals that control your skeletal muscles.

The grey matter is surrounded by white matter, which is packed with nerve fibres that help signals to travel up and down the spinal cord more quickly.

BRAIN

BRAINSTEM

SPINAL CORD
Stretches all the way down your back from your brain.

VERTEBRAE
Covering and protecting your spinal cord are a collection of bones called vertebrae. You're born with 33 of these bones, but by the time you're an adult you'll have 24 as some of the bones at the bottom end will have joined together.

SPINAL NERVES

A total of 31 pairs of spinal nerves branch out from the spinal cord to your upper and lower body. They carry instructions to and away from your spinal cord, helping you to feel and move your muscles.

DID YOU KNOW?

The spinal cord sends complex messages quickly to all parts of the body. This is why the most intelligent animals, including humans, apes and dolphins, have them. However, octopuses don't and yet they're some of the smartest animals in the world. Experiments have shown that they can solve puzzles, camouflage themselves and even tell the difference between individual humans.

NERVE CELLS

YOUR BODY'S WIRING SYSTEM

Nerve cells, or neurons, are like electrical wires. They're long and thin, and take information all around your body. They're made up of fibres and each one carries a separate electrical signal. Here's a look at their different parts and what they do.

NUCLEUS
The cell's control centre.

AXON
Carries outgoing signals to nearby nerve cells.

AXON TERMINAL
Connects with other cells to pass on signals.

CELL BODY
Contains the cell's nucleus.

DENDRITE
Receives and processes incoming signals.

TYPES OF NERVE CELL

You have three types of nerve cell. Sensory nerves send signals to the spinal cord and brain from sense receptors all over your body. Motor nerves send signals in the opposite direction, from your spinal cord and brain to your muscles and other body parts, telling them what to do. Mixed nerves do exactly what they sound like – a bit of both!

Some signals can travel at speeds of around 322 km (200 mi) per hour. That's the same as the top speed of a sports car.

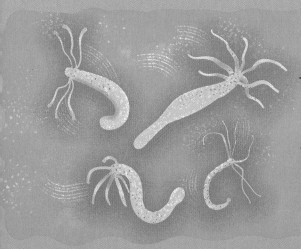

DID YOU KNOW?

The hydra, a tiny animal that lives in water, has the simplest nervous system of any animal. It has up to a few thousand nerve cells, whereas humans have an estimated 86 billion. Experts are amazed by how the hydra is able to survive, considering it has such a small number of nerve cells.

REFLEXES

Reflexes are movements that your muscles make and are controlled by your nerves. These automatic movements are usually to protect you. For example, you might move your hands to cover your face when a ball flies towards you.

TRY IT AT HOME: REFLEX TEST

1. Sit down on a surface where your legs dangle off the floor.
2. Gently hit the area just below your kneecap with the side of your hand.
3. Your leg should naturally kick forward slightly.

This reaction is called a knee-jerk reflex and it helps you to keep your balance. Doctors will sometimes use a small hammer to tap a tendon called the patellar, which is just below the knee and connected to your muscles. This gentle knock causes the leg muscles to contract and assures the doctor that your nervous system is working correctly.

4

THE SKELETAL SYSTEM

Your skeleton is your body's framework. It's made up of bones and the tissues that connect them, which include cartilage, tendons and ligaments.

Your skeletal system has a number of important jobs. Firstly, it supports your body and gives it its shape. It also protects delicate and vital body parts. For example, your ribs keep your heart and lungs safe, and your skull looks after your brain. Your skeleton is also connected to your muscles and both work together to allow movement.

It's time to find out all about your skeletal system.

YOUR SKELETON
THE BODY'S FRAMEWORK

Your skeleton is made up of 206 bones. Take a look at them and what they do.

ARMS

You have three bones in your arm: the humerus, radius and ulna.

SKULL

This protects your brain and gives your head its shape. However, it isn't just one bone but 22 different bones that fuse together after you're born. The bones inside a newborn's skull aren't fully formed, which is why babies have two soft patches on their heads.

RIBS

Your ribcage is made of 12 pairs of ribs. They support the chest and protect your heart and lungs.

DID YOU KNOW?

The humerus is often called the 'funny bone' because of the strange feeling you get when you hit it near your elbow. However, this has nothing to do with the bone itself, but a nerve called the ulnar nerve which runs down your arm past your elbow. Hitting this part of your arm knocks the nerve against the bone and gives you a strange tingling sensation.

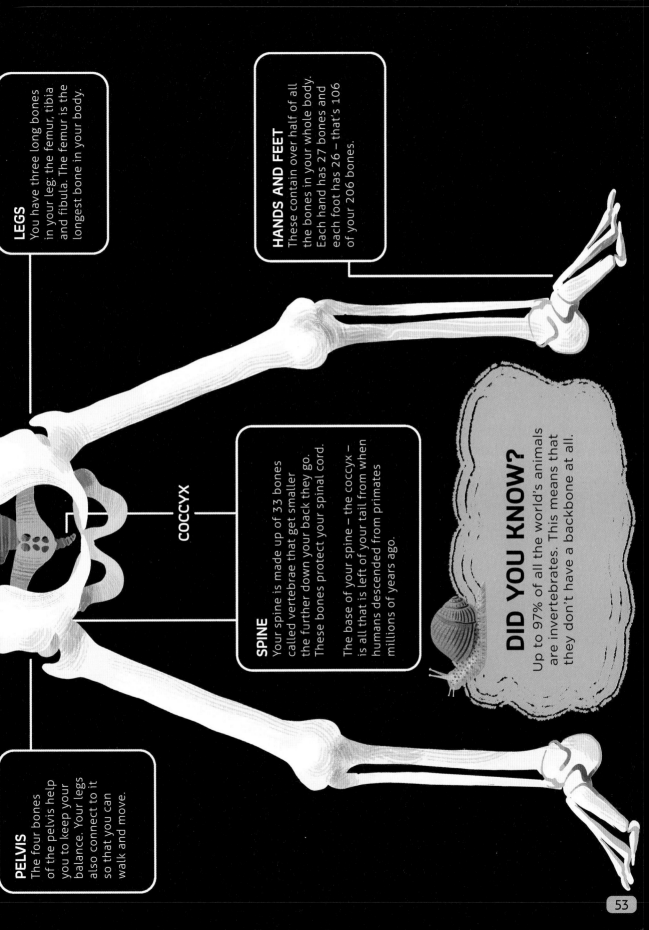

LEGS

You have three long bones in your leg: the femur, tibia and fibula. The femur is the longest bone in your body.

HANDS AND FEET

These contain over half of all the bones in your whole body. Each hand has 27 bones and each foot has 26 – that's 106 of your 206 bones.

COCCYX

SPINE

Your spine is made up of 33 bones called vertebrae that get smaller the further down your back they go. These bones protect your spinal cord.

The base of your spine – the coccyx – is all that is left of your tail from when humans descended from primates millions of years ago.

DID YOU KNOW?

Up to 97% of all the world's animals are invertebrates. This means that they don't have a backbone at all.

PELVIS

The four bones of the pelvis help you to keep your balance. Your legs also connect to it so that you can walk and move.

53

PULL YOURSELF TOGETHER

THE LIGAMENTS BETWEEN YOUR BONES

Ligaments are tough strands of tissue that connect your bones to one another and support your joints. You have over 900 ligaments within your body, including inside your arms, legs, feet and even your spine.

Glue

COLLAGEN

Ligaments are made from lots of bundles of collagen fibres. Collagen is a protein found in skin, bone, muscles, cartilage and tendons.

FLEXIBLE FEET

There are lots of ligaments attached to your ankle, heel and the sole of your foot. These allow the joints in your foot to move so that you can walk, run and stand on the tips of your toes. They also stop your bones from being pulled apart.

People whose bodies are very flexible, such as gymnasts and acrobats, have super-stretchy ligaments.

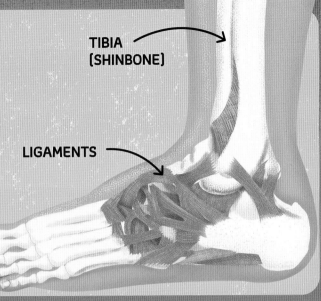

TIBIA (SHINBONE)

LIGAMENTS

THE FRONT OF YOUR SPINE

THE SIDE OF YOUR SPINE

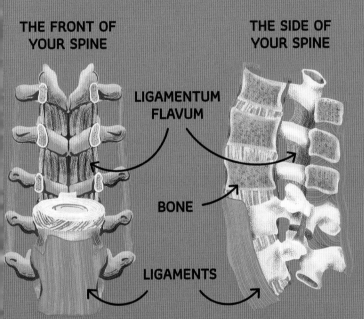

LIGAMENTUM FLAVUM

BONE

LIGAMENTS

YOUR SPINE

The individual bones of your spine are supported by ligaments. The diagrams opposite show a small section of your lower spine, the lumbar. Here, you can see the 'ligamentum flavum', the strongest type of ligament in your spine. It runs all the way from the base of your skull down to your pelvis and helps to protect the spinal cord and nerves.

DID YOU KNOW?

All of the bones inside your body are connected together either at one end or both. But there is one exception – the hyoid. This U-shaped bone plays a key role in moving your tongue, chewing, swallowing, coughing and speech.

HYOID BONE

THE WONDERS OF CARTILAGE

THE COATING THAT KEEPS YOU SMOOTH

The ends of your bones are coated in a tough but flexible material called cartilage, which protects and cushions your joints and bones. Cartilage is in lots of areas of your body, including your knees, nose and ears.

MUSCLE

FEMUR
(THIGHBONE)

KNEES

Your knee is the largest joint in your body and allows the leg to smoothly bend and straighten. Inside your knee, a layer of cartilage sits between the ends of the femur and the tibia. This softens the impact on your bones when you walk or run, which stops them from wearing away.

GROWTH PLATE
Where new cartilage is made in children's bodies.

CARTILAGE

TENDON

LIGAMENT

TIBIA
(SHINBONE)

HOW IS CARTILAGE MADE?

When you're born, your bones are mostly made of cartilage. As you get older, this cartilage is replaced by bone tissue. At the end of long bones, such as your femur, there are sections called growth plates. Until your teens this is where cartilage is made, which then hardens into new bone.

NOSE AND EARS

While most of your cartilage is deep inside your body, you can feel the cartilage on your skull. Your nose and ears are mostly made of cartilage, which is why they're soft and flexible. You may have noticed that the skull on a skeleton doesn't have a nose or ears. This is because cartilage breaks down with other body tissues, such as muscle, when a body decays.

CARTILAGE

WHOOOSH!

DID YOU KNOW?

A shark's skeleton is made entirely of cartilage and so the joints that connect its jaws are very flexible. Some sharks, such as the great white shark, can push their jaws out to take enormous bites. This gives them a better chance at catching their prey and holding on to it.

5

THE RESPIRATORY AND CIRCULATORY SYSTEMS

The movement of blood and the movement of air inside your body are very closely connected. In fact, one of the main jobs of your blood is to carry oxygen from your lungs to all of the other parts of your body. You can feel this process happening when you exercise. When you're physically active, your heart starts to beat faster and stronger as it pumps blood more quickly around your body. You also breathe more deeply and more often as your lungs take in more air to get all of the oxygen that your body needs to keep working.

This chapter explores both your respiratory system, which is made up of your airways, lungs and blood vessels, and your circulatory system, which consists of your heart, blood and blood vessels.

YOUR RESPIRATORY SYSTEM

THE BODY'S AIRWAYS

Your airways take in air and provide oxygen to your blood. This diagram shows the passage of air through your body.

MOUTH AND NOSE
These are the two main ways for air to get in and out of your body. They're connected at the back of your throat.

POP!

BREATHING IN AND OUT

The diaphragm is a sheet of muscle that helps to inflate your lungs during breathing. When you breathe in, your diaphragm tightens and pulls down. At the same time, your rib muscles tighten and pull your ribcage up and out. This makes your chest bigger and so your lungs expand to fill the empty space.

When you breathe out, your diaphragm relaxes, and goes back to its natural, curved shape, which pushes up against the lungs. At the same time, your rib muscles relax and your ribcage shrinks back down and in. As a result, air is forced back out of your body.

WHAT IS AIR?

Air is made up of the gases that surround our planet. It's mostly nitrogen (78%) and oxygen (21%) as well as small amounts of other gases, including carbon dioxide (0.04%). However, oxygen is the only gas from this mixture that your body actually uses.

AIR SACS

LUNG

DID YOU KNOW?

Birds have air sacs throughout their bodies, even in their bottoms, which transfer air to their lungs so that there is always a constant supply. This explains how they're able to get enough energy to power themselves into the air.

THROAT
Connects your nose and mouth to your windpipe.

VOICE BOX
Contains your vocal cords.

WINDPIPE
Carries air to and from the lungs.

LUNG
Two lungs get oxygen into – and carbon dioxide out of – your blood.

HEART
Pumps blood to the lungs to pick up oxygen.

RIBS
Protect the lungs.

DIAPHRAGM
Helps to inflate and deflate the lungs during breathing.

INSIDE YOUR LUNGS

THE TRANSFER OF OXYGEN INTO THE BLOOD

Inside your lungs, oxygen enters the bloodstream and carbon dioxide is removed. Here's a closer look at the inside of your lungs, their different parts and what they do.

RIGHT BRONCHUS
Carries air to and from the right lung.

WINDPIPE
Takes air to and from the lungs.

LEFT BRONCHUS
Carries air to and from the left lung.

PULMONARY ARTERY
Moves blood into the lungs.

PULMONARY VEIN
Moves oxygenated blood out of the lungs.

BRONCHIOLES
These are smaller branches from the bronchi (plural of bronchus). There are around 30,000 bronchioles in each lung.

HEART
Your heart sits behind your left lung. This is why your left lung is slightly smaller than your right.

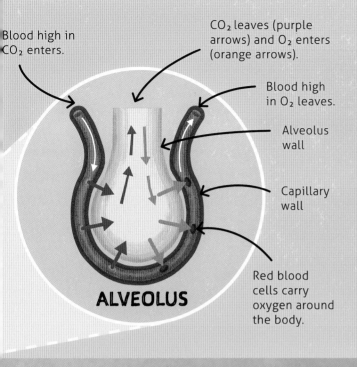

Blood high in CO₂ enters.

CO₂ leaves (purple arrows) and O₂ enters (orange arrows).

Blood high in O₂ leaves.

Alveolus wall

Capillary wall

Red blood cells carry oxygen around the body.

ALVEOLUS

ALVEOLI AND GAS EXCHANGE

At the end of each bronchiole are tiny sacs of air called alveoli (plural of alveolus). These make the transfer of oxygen into your blood possible. The alveoli are surrounded by blood vessels called capillaries. When you breathe in, oxygen (O_2) passes through the alveolus and capillary walls into the blood. This process is known as a gas exchange. It works the other way, too. When you breathe out, carbon dioxide (CO_2) leaves the blood and is passed out through your lungs and back into the air.

TRY IT AT HOME: MAKE A MODEL LUNG

Creating a model lung is a great way to understand more about the respiratory system and how your lungs work. You'll need a large plastic bottle, a pair of scissors and two balloons.

1. Using a pair of scissors, cut off the bottom of a bottle, leaving the neck and main body.

2. Place one balloon inside the bottle and then fold the lip of the balloon around the lid so that it hangs down from the top.

3. Tie a knot in the bottom of a second balloon and cut the top off of it.

4. Stretch the cut part of the balloon over the bottom of the bottle.

5. Now to test it. As you pull down on the knot of the balloon, it will cause the balloon inside to inflate.

This is what happens to your lungs when you breathe in. And when you let go of the knot, the balloon will deflate. This is what happens when you breathe out and air is expelled (let out) from your lungs.

YOUR CIRCULATORY SYSTEM

BLOOD'S JOURNEY AROUND YOUR BODY

This system is all about your heart and blood vessels, which work together to keep blood flowing around your body. Blood feeds your cells oxygen, which keeps them alive. This diagram shows the main parts of the circulatory system and what they do.

BLOOD VESSELS

There are three types of blood vessel. Arteries take blood away from the heart and veins carry blood back to the heart. Capillaries connect arteries and veins.

AROUND THE WORLD

Your body contains 96,560 km (60,000 mi) of blood vessels. That's more than twice the distance around the world!

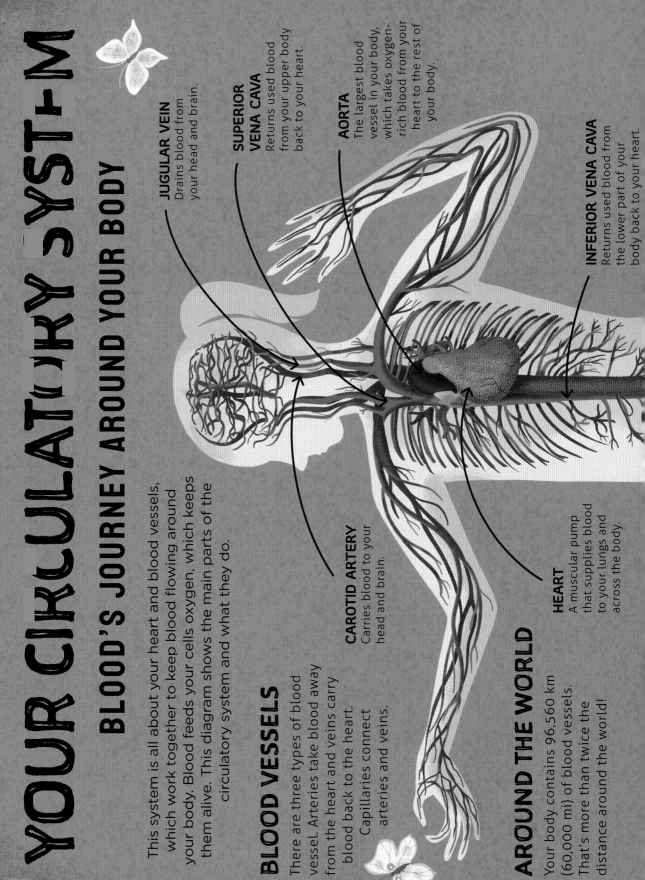

JUGULAR VEIN
Drains blood from your head and brain.

SUPERIOR VENA CAVA
Returns used blood from your upper body back to your heart.

AORTA
The largest blood vessel in your body, which takes oxygen-rich blood from your heart to the rest of your body.

INFERIOR VENA CAVA
Returns used blood from the lower part of your body back to your heart.

CAROTID ARTERY
Carries blood to your head and brain.

HEART
A muscular pump that supplies blood to your lungs and across the body.

DID YOU KNOW?

Zebrafish are able to regrow the tissue in their bodies, including their hearts. They can lose up to 20% of their heart muscle without it affecting their survival and can repair the damage within eight weeks.

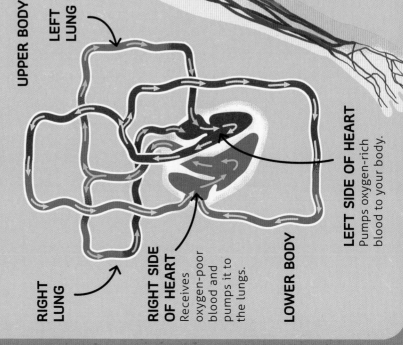

Tiny blood vessels run throughout your body, all the way to the tips of your fingers and toes.

THE TWO-LOOP SYSTEM

The diagram below shows how blood travels around your body in one direction through two loops, which are linked by the heart.

The shorter loop (green arrows) carries blood to your lungs where it picks up oxygen. This blood then travels around the longer loop (yellow arrows), dropping off oxygen around the body in arteries before returning back to the heart.

UPPER BODY

LEFT LUNG

RIGHT LUNG

RIGHT SIDE OF HEART
Receives oxygen-poor blood and pumps it to the lungs.

LOWER BODY

LEFT SIDE OF HEART
Pumps oxygen-rich blood to your body.

INSIDE YOUR HEART

YOUR BODY'S ENGINE ROOM

Your heart is at the centre of your circulatory system and beats every second to pump blood around your body. Here's a closer look at what goes on inside your heart.

SUPERIOR VENA CAVA

AORTA

PULMONARY ARTERIES
Carry blood away from your heart towards the lungs.

ATRIUMS
Your heart has two atriums. The right atrium receives blood that's low in oxygen from the body. The left atrium receives oxygenated blood from the lungs via the pulmonary veins.

HEARTSTRINGS
These thin tendon-like cords secure the valve between each atrium and ventricle.

PULMONARY VEINS
Carry blood from the lungs to the heart.

WALL OF MUSCLE
Divides the heart into left and right halves.

PERICARDIUM
A double-layered sac-like tissue membrane that protects the heart.

VALVES
Your heart has four valves, which open and close during each heartbeat to make sure that blood always travels in the right direction. This arrow is pointing to the pulmonary valve.

INFERIOR VENA CAVA

VENTRICLES
Your right ventricle carries blood to the pulmonary artery, on the way to your lungs. Your left ventricle pushes blood into the aorta for sending out into your body.

HEARTBEAT AND PULSE

Every heartbeat forces blood into your arteries, which makes them bulge. This bulging sensation is your pulse, which you can feel on the inside of your wrist and neck. When relaxed, most adults' hearts beat 60–100 times per minute.

The diagrams below show what happens inside your heart every time it beats.

To test your pulse, lightly press your index (first) finger and middle finger on the inside of the top of your wrist. Can you count the beats?

STAGE 1
When the heart muscle relaxes, blood flows into the right and left atria (plural of atrium). Oxygen-poor blood enters the right atrium and oxygen-rich blood enters the left atrium.

STAGE 2
The walls of each atrium tighten to push blood through a valve into the ventricles, which fill with blood.

STAGE 3
The walls of the ventricles squeeze to push the blood through valves into the arteries. Oxygen-poor blood is forced into your lungs and oxygen-rich blood is carried around the rest of your body.

ZZZZ!

DID YOU KNOW?
Some animals hibernate during the winter months when food is scarce. In order to preserve energy, their heartbeats slow right down. Wood frogs in Alaska, North America, actually freeze over for up to eight months during the winter. While frozen, their hearts don't beat at all and when spring arrives, the frogs thaw (defrost) and hop away.

INSIDE YOUR BLOOD

THE INGREDIENTS THAT MAKE UP YOUR BLOOD

BLOOD VESSEL

Your blood is made up of trillions of cells that float in a liquid called plasma. Not only do these cells carry the vital oxygen that your body needs, they also transport nutrients and fight germs.

RED BLOOD CELLS
Contain a protein called haemoglobin, which picks up oxygen inside the lungs. Your blood carries these cells to the rest of your body and releases the oxygen so that it can be used by your other cells. About 40–45% of your blood is made up of red blood cells.

PLASMA
Contains the nutrients needed to keep your cells alive, including sugars, fats, proteins and salts.

PLATELETS
Rush towards a bleeding part of the body to form a plug. This is known as a blood clot, which stops you from bleeding.

HEAT
Your blood also gives out heat, keeping your body at a constant temperature.

WHITE BLOOD CELLS
Protect your body against germs by absorbing them and releasing chemicals to break them down and destroy them.

DID YOU KNOW?

There are four main blood groups: A, B, AB and O. Your blood group is determined by the genes you inherit from your parents. Blood group O is the most common and is used in blood transfusions when a patient's blood type is unknown.

WHERE DOES BLOOD COME FROM?

Inside the middle of your bones is a soft, spongy tissue called bone marrow. This produces 'stem cells', which are the building blocks that the body uses to make blood cells.

Most of your bones contain bone marrow. However, by the time you're an adult, only the bones of your skull, spine, ribs and hips, and the long bones of your arms and legs, will contain bone marrow. This is because as you grow old the number of red and white blood cells and platelets in your blood decreases.

BONE

BLOOD
VESSELS

BONE
MARROW

6

THE DIGESTIVE SYSTEM

Your digestive system breaks food down into chemicals called nutrients, which your body uses to grow, repair and keep itself working. These are absorbed into the bloodstream, while any waste that can't be digested is removed. This system is made up of a long, twisting tube called the digestive tract. Its main parts are the oesophagus, stomach, small intestine and large intestine. Other organs, including the liver and the pancreas, also play a key role in the digestion process.

In this chapter, you'll explore the important role of each part and how they help to digest your food.

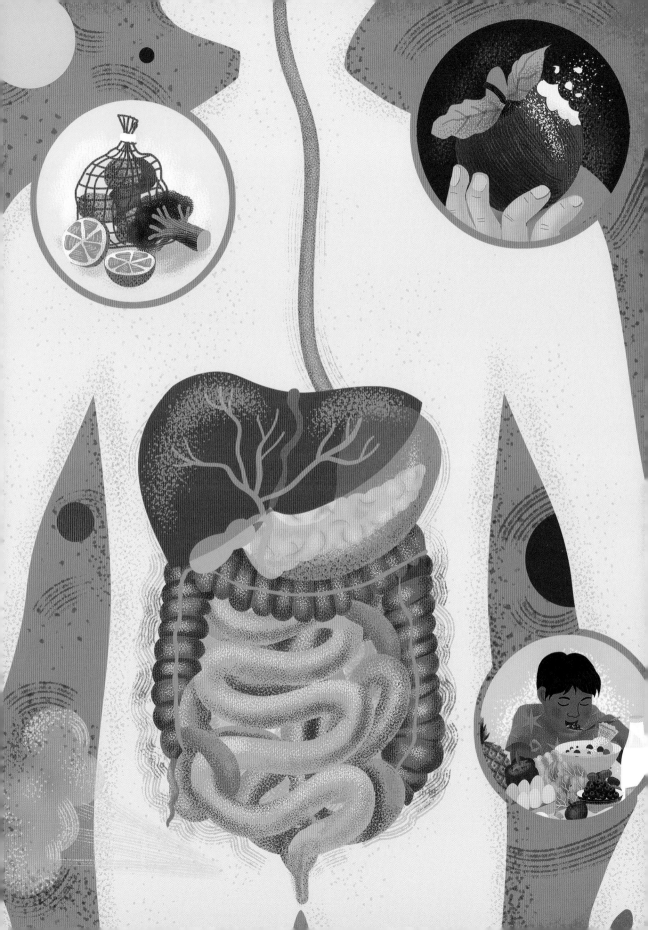

GLUG!

WATER AND FOOD

THE BODY'S FUEL

Your body needs water and food so that it can get the nutrients required for growth and keep all of its parts working properly.

WATER

Water is essential for life and every living organism relies on it. In fact, scientists exploring space will often use the presence of water as a sign that a planet might have life on it. You should be drinking around six to eight glasses of water a day. Here's why:

The blood in your body is around 50% water so you need plenty of it to keep your blood and cells working properly.

Water helps make saliva in your mouth, which breaks down the food you eat.

Your kidneys and bowels need water to flush out waste, such as urine (wee) and faeces (poo).

Your cartilage, which helps to lubricate your bones, contains around 80% water.

If you fancy some flavour, most fruits and vegetables contain lots of water. Apples are 86% water and cucumbers are 96% water.

DID YOU KNOW?

The kangaroo rat can survive its entire life without drinking water. It still needs water to live, but absorbs it from the seeds that it eats. It lives in the deserts of Arizona, USA, where there is very little water available.

A BALANCED DIET

Different foods provide different nutrients, so in order to stay healthy you need variety in your diet. Here's a look at the five main food groups and why they're important.

CARBOHYDRATES

Bread and other starchy foods, such as potatoes, are the main source of energy for your body's cells, tissues and organs.

DAIRY

Milk, cheese and yoghurt are a good source of calcium, which is needed for maintaining healthy bones.

FRUITS AND VEGETABLES

These contain vitamins and minerals. Oranges are a good source of vitamin C, which helps to fight infections. Broccoli contains iron, which your body needs to make blood.

PROTEINS

Meat, fish, eggs and nuts are high in protein, which is important for cell growth and repair.

FATS AND SUGARS

Nuts, oils and avocados are high in fat, and fruits are high in sugar. These provide energy.

DID YOU KNOW?

A lot of the minerals that your body needs come from the soils that grow fruit and vegetables, which absorb the minerals as they grow. However, getting these important nutrients isn't so easy for some animals. Ibex goats have to climb incredibly steep cliffs just to lick the salt and minerals that trickle from the rocks!

INSIDE YOUR MOUTH

WHERE DIGESTION BEGINS

The first stage of digestion begins in your mouth. Here, your teeth, tongue and salivary glands work together to break up your food so that it can be swallowed. The diagram below shows the different parts of your mouth and what they do.

SALIVARY GLANDS

You have three pairs of salivary glands inside your mouth that release saliva. One pair sits under your tongue and another below your jaw. The parotid glands are your largest salivary glands and are located in front of your ears. All three pairs are shown in purple.

TEETH
Cut up your food as it enters your mouth, and chew and grind to break it down.

TONGUE
Not only does your tongue have taste buds, it also moves your food around your mouth and between your teeth.

THROAT
Connects your mouth and nose to your oesophagus.

EPIGLOTTIS
This sheet of cartilage stops food from going down your windpipe when swallowing, otherwise you'd choke.

WINDPIPE
Carries air from your nose and mouth to your lungs.

OESOPHAGUS
Carries food from your throat to your stomach.

YOUR SALIVA

While you eat, your food is moistened with saliva, which makes it wet and mushy so that it's easier to swallow. Your saliva contains enzymes which are proteins that help to break down your food even more. Once broken down, the nutrients inside your food are passed into the bloodstream and sent around the body.

TRY IT AT HOME: MAKE A MODEL DIGESTIVE SYSTEM (PART 1)

Throughout this chapter, you can copy the stages that your body goes through when you digest your food. Follow the instructions below to start the process:

1. Get a large, resealable, clear plastic bag.

2. Using your hands, rip up a piece of bread into small chunks and drop it into the bag.

3. Add some milk (milk contains one of the same enzymes found in saliva).

4. Seal the bag and squeeze the contents with your hands.

Now you've got a wet bready mush, which is exactly what the food in your mouth looks like before you swallow it – delicious!

Turn the page to find out what happens when it reaches your stomach and look at the instructions for Part 2.

DID YOU KNOW?

Burmese pythons are among the largest snakes on Earth. They have elastic-like jaws which allow them to swallow animals up to five times as wide as their head, such as goats and pigs. They swallow them whole, too, unlike humans who cut up and chew their food.

INSIDE YOUR STOMACH

YOUR BODY'S BLENDER

Once your food has been broken down and swallowed,
it travels through your oesophagus and into your stomach.
Here, your food is stored and only part-digested.

MIX AND MASH

It's the stomach's job to break down your food into a liquid and release it at a steady rate so that the small intestine has time to digest it.

The diagram opposite shows the main parts of the stomach and what they do.

OESOPHAGUS
Waves of muscle contractions in the oesophagus push your food into your stomach.

PROTECTIVE LAYER
An outer layer of tissue covers the stomach to separate it from your other organs.

MUSCLE LAYERS
Three layers of muscle cross over one another in different directions. These squeeze to churn up your food.

TRY IT AT HOME: MAKE A MODEL DIGESTIVE SYSTEM (PART 2)

To see what happens inside your stomach, you need to add some acid to your chewed-up food:

1. Unseal the bag and add two tablespoons of vinegar or lemon juice to the mixture (the acidity of these is similar to the gastric acid inside your stomach, but not as strong).

2. Seal up the bag again and squash its contents.

3. Leave the bag for ten minutes.

You should now have a creamy, bready soup, which is similar to the chyme in your stomach. Turn the page to find out what happens when your food reaches your intestines, and see the instructions for Part 3.

VALVE
Where chyme leaves the stomach and enters the small intestine.

PYLORIC SPHINCTER
A ring of muscle at the exit of the stomach, which opens to release chyme.

GASTRIC PITS
Entrances to the gastric glands which release gastric acid and enzymes that break down your food.

CHYME
When your food is mixed with gastric acid and enzymes, it becomes a liquid mush called chyme.

FULL AND EMPTY

Filling and emptying your stomach can take up to four hours. Here's what happens:

While you eat, your stomach fills and expands. Its walls contract to mix chewed-up food with gastric acid and enzymes.

Between one and two hours after eating, your food is partly digested by gastric juice and mixed by even more powerful contractions into chyme.

Between three and four hours after eating, the pyloric sphincter opens and the stomach wall contracts to push a bit of chyme into the small intestine. This process repeats several times.

INSIDE YOUR INTESTINES

WHERE DIGESTION ENDS

Most of your food is digested by your small intestine, while your large intestine absorbs water from waste to form faeces (poo).

SMALL INTESTINE

At around 7 m (23 ft) long, your small intestine is taller than a giraffe! It is coiled up to fit inside your abdomen. Like the stomach, it produces enzymes which help to break down chyme even more. It also absorbs nutrients from your food so that they can be used by your body's cells.

☐ **SMALL INTESTINE**

☐ **LARGE INTESTINE**

LARGE INTESTINE

This is twice the width of the small intestine, but only 1.5 m (5 ft) long. Its walls soak up water and vitamins from undigested food. Three of its main parts are the caecum, colon and rectum.

1. STOMACH

2. DUODENUM

The first part of the small intestine, where enzymes are mixed with chyme and more nutrients are absorbed.

3. VILLI

Thousands of tiny bumps line the inside of the small intestine, which increase the surface area to help speed up the absorption of nutrients.

PFFFT!

6. COLON
Removes water and some nutrients from food. Contractions also push food waste towards the rectum.

7. RECTUM
A storage area for faeces. Any remaining water is absorbed and the faeces harden.

4. VALVE
Here, chyme is passed from the small intestine to the large intestine.

5. CAECUM
The first part of your large intestine, which connects the small intestine to your colon.

BRAAAP!

8. ANUS
Faeces leave your body through the anus.

TRY IT AT HOME: MAKE A MODEL DIGESTIVE SYSTEM (PART 3)

In the final phase of your DIY digestion journey, you've reached the intestines and it's now time to make some poo ...

1. Unseal the bag again and pour the chyme from the bag through a muslin cloth (or dishcloth) and into a bowl.

2. Squeeze the cloth to get as much liquid as possible out of it (this is similar to what happens inside your intestines).

3. When you have a lump of damp bread left in the muslin, use some kitchen towel to pat it and squeeze it even more.

4. Eventually, you won't be able to squeeze any more liquid out of the waste.

Now you're left with a lump of waste product similar to poo!

INSIDE YOUR LIVER AND PANCREAS

PROCESSING YOUR BODY'S NUTRIENTS

Once the nutrients from your food have been absorbed, they're carried around your body by your blood. First, however, your liver and pancreas turn these nutrients into the chemicals that the body needs to function.

LIVER
Your largest internal organ is your liver and it does around 500 different jobs, including processing the nutrients released from your food.

It breaks down food and converts it into energy, it helps the body to get rid of waste and it plays a key role in fighting infection.

OESOPHAGUS

GALL BLADDER
Stores bile – a green fluid from the liver which turns fats into tiny droplets that are easier to break down and digest – and then releases it.

STOMACH

BILE DUCT
Collects and carries bile from the cells of the liver.

SMALL INTESTINE

PANCREAS
The intestine releases hormones when food enters it, which causes the pancreas to create enzymes. These help to digest fats, sugars, carbohydrates and proteins. The pancreas also produces hormones called insulin and glucagon, which control the amount of sugar in the blood.

INSULIN

Glucose is the main source of energy for your body's cells. Insulin moves through the bloodstream and helps your cells take the glucose they need from your blood. Glucagon does the opposite and causes the liver to add glucose to the blood.

Some people have diabetes, which means their body has a problem producing insulin. They use glucose monitors, which are connected to a sensor in the arm or abdomen, and measure the levels of glucose in their blood.

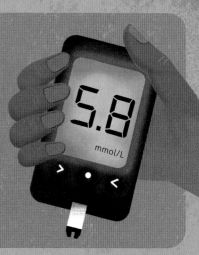

5.8 mmol/L

THE URINARY SYSTEM

Your kidneys help to process your body's blood, removing excess fluid and waste, which is carried to the bladder and flushed out of the body through your urethra.

1. KIDNEYS
Clean your blood and filter out waste through your urine.

2. URETERS
Two ureters carry urine from the kidneys to the bladder.

3. BLADDER
Stores urine until the bladder sends messages to the brain telling it that it needs to be emptied.

4. URETHRA
A tube that carries urine out of the body.

Shown here is the female urinary system, which has a short urethra. The male system is the same, but the urethra is longer and passes along the penis.

DID YOU KNOW?
The amount of blood that passes through the kidneys in a single lifetime could fill an estimated 18 Olympic-sized swimming pools!

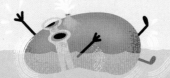

7

BRILLIANT ANIMAL BODIES

Now that you've explored how extraordinary the human body is, it's time to find out how amazing other animals' bodies are. From special skeletons and brilliant blood to super senses and spectacular speeds, these creatures have some pretty cool features that make them perfectly adapted to the lives they lead. Welcome to the wonderful world of awesome animal bodies!

EXOSKELETONS

NOT ALL SKELETONS LOOK THE SAME

Exoskeletons are hard outer shells that support and protect the insides of some animals. Invertebrates (animals without backbones) are the largest group of animals, and many of them have exoskeletons. Look below and find out some of their uses and advantages.

SUIT OF ARMOUR

The hard covering of an exoskeleton protects the internal organs of the animals that have them. This makes it difficult for predators to pierce their skin, kill and eat them.

GRASSHOPPER

GREAT FOR MOVEMENT

The individual parts of an exoskeleton are strong and stiff. However, they have joints which allow them to move just like your skeleton.

RHINOCEROS BEETLE

RAINCOAT

Exoskeletons are waterproof so they block rainwater from getting inside animals' bodies. They also stop moisture escaping, which helps to prevent animals from drying out.

PRAYING MANTIS

SHELLS

Some animals, such as oysters and snails, have a special type of exoskeleton called a shell. This is made of a substance called calcium carbonate. As the soft tissues of their bodies grow, so do their shells.

NUMBERS

New animals are being discovered every day and those with exoskeletons are found most often. Experts estimate that for every human being on Earth, there are around 1.4 billion insects.

ARACHNIDS
It has been estimated that there are around 600,000 different species of arachnids, which includes scorpions and spiders.

INSECTS
Scientists have discovered over 1 million species of insects, but estimate that there could be as many as 10 million. Insects include butterflies, beetles and ants.

CRUSTACEANS
There are around 42,000 different species of crustaceans, including crabs, shrimps and lobsters.

DID YOU KNOW?

When an animal gets too big, its exoskeleton splits open and falls off. This process is called moulting. Look around your house and you might spot what looks like a dead spider with its legs curled up. This isn't actually a dead spider, but an old exoskeleton.

BRILLIANT BLOOD

THE DIFFERENT TYPES OF BLOOD IN THE ANIMAL KINGDOM

Animals have different body temperatures depending on where they live. Some are able to regulate their own body temperatures, while others aren't. Find out the differences between them below.

WARM-BLOODED

Nearly all birds and mammals, including humans, are warm-blooded. This means that their bodies work hard to maintain the same temperature all the time. When it's really cold their bodies shiver, and this quick movement of their muscles generates heat. Some animals have a thick layer of fur or fat to keep them warm. Whales have a layer of fat called blubber, which helps them to survive in water temperatures as cold as 4°C (39°F).

COLD-BLOODED

Some animals, such as fish, reptiles and insects, are cold-blooded and can't generate their own body heat. To regulate their body temperature, they need to move to different environments.

Crocodiles will bask in the Sun to warm up their blood. One advantage of being cold-blooded is that these animals don't need as much energy, and therefore can survive on less food. Crocodiles can go without food for several months.

AMBUSHING

Many cold-blooded animals don't chase their prey as this uses up a lot of energy. Instead, they hide and wait. When something delicious comes along, they jump out and grab it. This technique is called ambushing and lots of animals rely on it to survive.

Lizards spend most of their time sitting on branches, hiding behind leaves, and use their long, sticky tongues to catch their prey.

RAINBOW BLOOD

The colour of an animal's blood is determined by the minerals inside it and what happens when they combine with oxygen.

RED BLOOD
In humans, a protein called haemoglobin carries oxygen around the body in the bloodstream. Haemoglobin contains iron which mixes with oxygen to make a red colour.

PURPLE BLOOD
Some worms that live in water have a protein in their blood which makes it turn purple when it combines with oxygen. Before it mixes, the blood is colourless.

BLUE BLOOD
Spiders, crustaceans and some octopuses have a copper protein in their blood. When this combines with oxygen it turns blue.

GREEN BLOOD
Some marine worms have a chemical in their blood that goes bright green when it combines with oxygen.

SUPER SENSES

ANIMALS WITH INCREDIBLE SENSES

Some animals have amazing senses and there are even animals with extra senses that humans don't have. This means they experience the world in ways we can't even imagine.

SUPER SIGHT

The bald eagle has vision that is eight times more powerful than a human's, thanks to a very dense coating of light-detecting cells on its retinas. This means that when it's flying it can see prey from over 3 km (2 mi) away. That's like spotting your lunch on the ground from more than halfway up Mount Kilimanjaro.

NOSE RAY
This mole's nostrils are ringed by 22 nose rays.

SMELLING UNDERWATER

The star-nosed mole is one of the only animals that can smell underwater. It does this by breathing out small bubbles of air, which pick up odour molecules, then catching them with its nose rays and breathing them back in. This enables the mole to smell its prey, even in the darkest depths of the bogs and marshes where it lives.

ECHOES IN THE DARK

Some animals, such as bats and dolphins, find food in the dark and underwater through 'echolocation'. This is a technique that uses echoes to determine the location of things. These animals make sounds that travel through the air or water. When the echo of that noise bounces off prey, the animal is able to work out where it is from the resulting echo. Bats use their giant ears to hear these echoes.

ELECTRIC BURSTS

'Electroreception' is the ability to feel little electric bursts underwater. Sharks have lots of little pores all over their heads called ampullae of Lorenzini, which are filled with mucus. These detect the electrical currents produced by other animals as they move and so help sharks to locate their prey.

INCREDIBLE NOSES

It might not be surprising when you look at their great big trunks, but elephants have one of the best senses of smell in the animal kingdom. They can smell water up to 19 km (12 mi) away, helping them to find places to drink in the hot countries where they live.

AMAZING ANIMAL BODIES

RECORD-BREAKING BEASTS AND THEIR HUMAN COUNTERPARTS

Welcome to the Animal Hall of Fame. Discover how humans compare to the strongest, fastest, tallest and oldest animals that have ever lived.

SPEED MACHINES

The fastest land animal is a cheetah, which can run up to 120 km (75 mi) per hour. In fact, it can accelerate from 0 to 97 km (60 mi) per hour in only three seconds – that's faster than most cars.

Usain Bolt recorded the fastest-ever time for a human. In 2009, he ran 100 m (328 ft) in 9.58 seconds. During this race, he reached a top speed of 44.72 km (27.79 mi) per hour.

DID YOU KNOW?

Not everyone can be the oldest, strongest, tallest or fastest person in the world. However, when you were born, for a split second YOU were the youngest person alive. You're a champion!

LASTING LEGENDS

The longest-living land animal is a giant tortoise named Jonathan. In 2022, he celebrated his 190th birthday. This means that Jonathan has lived through the Victorian era, the first Moon landing in 1969 and the invention of the internet.

The longest-living human ever recorded was Jeanne Louise Calment, who lived for 122 years and 164 days. Jeanne is known as a 'supercentenarian', a title given to people who reach the age of 110 years old.

JUMBO GIANTS

Unsurprisingly, a giraffe is the tallest animal ever recorded. A male Masai giraffe, named George, stood at 5.8 m (19 ft) tall.

George was more than twice the height of the tallest human ever recorded, Robert Wadlow. Robert was 2.72 m (8 ft and 11.1 in) tall.

TOUGH TITANS

Dung beetles are one of the strongest animals and can pull 1,141 times their own body weight. That's the same as an average-sized human pulling along six double-decker buses full of people.

In January 2015, Hafþór Björnsson broke a 1,000-year-old record by walking five steps with a 650-kg (1,433-lb) log on his back. That's the equivalent of carrying more than four adult pandas.

GLOSSARY

Here are some of the words used in this book.
You might want to remind yourself what they mean.
Words in italics are explained elsewhere in the glossary.

Alveoli
Tiny air sacs in your lungs where the lungs and blood exchange oxygen and carbon dioxide.

Aorta
The main artery that carries blood away from your heart to the rest of your body.

Bone marrow
A soft tissue inside your bones that produces new blood cells.

Brainstem
An area at the base of your brain that connects your *cerebrum* and your *spinal cord*.

Cartilage
A strong, flexible material that can be found inside your body, especially around your joints and in your nose and ears.

Cerebellum
The part of your brain that controls your body's movements and balance.

Cerebrum
The part of your brain that is responsible for your personality, preferences and emotions.

Chromosome
A thread-like structure of *DNA* found in the nucleus of most cells. Each cell in your body contains 46 chromosomes (23 pairs).

Cochlea
The spiral-shaped part of your inner ear. Tiny hair cells inside the cochlea turn vibrations into electrical impulses that travel to the brain.

Diabetes
A medical condition where someone has too much sugar in their blood.

Diaphragm
A sheet of muscle between your lungs and your stomach that's used when you breathe.

DNA
DNA is short for 'deoxyribonucleic acid'. It contains instructions that control how your cells work and how your body develops.

Echolocation
A system used by some animals, such as bats, to locate the position of an object by seeing how long it takes for sound waves to bounce off the object.

Electroreception
A system used by some animals, such as sharks, to locate the position of an object or prey by detecting eletrical signals.

Embryo
An organism, such as an unborn human or animal, in the very early stages of development.

Enamel
A hard, white substance that forms the outer part of your teeth.

Enzyme
A chemical substance that speeds up the reaction in a chemical process. For example, the saliva in your mouth contains enzymes which help to break down your food.

Epiglottis
A thin flap of tissue that covers the entrance to your voice box during swallowing, which stops food from entering your windpipe.

Exoskeleton
A hard external skeleton that protects the body of many animals, including insects.

Fertilization
When a female egg and a male sperm join together to create a new living being.

Gene
A section of *DNA* that controls what type of characteristics an animal or plant will have. Genes are passed from parents to child.

Genitalia
The organs of the human reproductive system.

Glucose
A type of sugar that gives you energy.

Grey matter
Grey-coloured tissue inside your brain and spinal cord that contains nerve cells.

Haemoglobin
A substance inside your blood that combines with oxygen and carries it around your body.

Hibernation
A way for some animals to cope with the cold of winter. Their body temperature drops and their breathing slows down so that they enter a state of deep sleep.

Hippocampus
An area inside your brain that is associated with memory and learning.

Hormone
A chemical that tells your cells, tissues and organs to do certain things.

Humerus
The upper bone of your arm which connects your shoulder to your elbow.

Insulin
The *hormone* that helps to control the level of *glucose* in your blood.

Invertebrate
An animal without a spine, such as a jellyfish.

Ligament
A tough band of tissue that connects your bones and joints. It also supports your organs.

Melanin
A pigment that gives your skin, hair and eyes their colour.

Nucleus
The centre of an animal cell, which controls the cell's growth and reproduction.

Organ
A part of your body that has a particular function. Your heart, for example, pumps blood around your body.

Paresthesia
An unusual tickling or tingling sensation in the skin, normally felt in the fingers, hands, arms, legs or feet.

Plasma
The clear liquid part of your blood that contains blood cells.

Platelet
A type of blood cell that helps to form a blood clot to stop bleeding and help heal wounds.

Puberty
The stage in life when your body starts becoming physically mature and transforms into an adult.

Reflex
An automatic reaction of your body to something that you feel, see or experience.

Retina
The area at the back of your eye, which receives the image that you see and sends it to your brain as an electrical signal.

Spinal cord
A thick cord of nerves inside your spine, which connects your brain to the nerves in the rest of your body.

Supercentenarian
A person who has reached the age of 110 years old.

Tendon
A cord-like structure that connects a muscle to a bone.

Vertebrae
The collection of bones inside your back that make up your spinal column, which covers and protects your *spinal cord* and nerves.

Vitreous humor
A clear, gel-like substance that helps to maintain the round shape of your eye and fills the space between the lens and the retina.

MEASUREMENTS

Here's a reminder of the metric and imperial measurements from inside this book.

Metric

Millimetre: mm
Centimetre: cm
Metre: m
Kilometre: km
Gram: g
Kilogram: kg
Tonne: t
Degree Celsius: °C

Imperial

Inch: in
Foot: ft
Mile: mi
Pound: lb
Ton: t
Degree Fahrenheit: °F

INDEX